His Journal, My Stella

poems by

Emily Bowles

Finishing Line Press
Georgetown, Kentucky

His Journal, My Stella

Copyright © 2018 by Emily Bowles
ISBN 978-1-63534-752-4 First Edition
All rights reserved under International and Pan-American Copyright Conventions. No part of this book may be reproduced in any manner whatsoever without written permission from the publisher, except in the case of brief quotations embodied in critical articles and reviews.

ACKNOWLEDGMENTS

These poems have appeared in print, some in slightly different forms:

"What Was Inserted," in *The Literary Nest* (Fall 2017).
"You See Me, a Woman Flayed," in *The Moon Magazine* (September 2017).
"Cedar Waxwing in Our House," in *Peacock Journal* (August 2017).
"De-Extinction Machines," in *Eye to the Telescope* (October 2017).

Publisher: Leah Maines
Editor: Christen Kincaid
Cover Art: *Blumenast* (branch in bloom). Acrylic on Canvas 2015.
    Artwork by Tanja Mona.
Author Photo: Nikki Kallio. Instagram: @NikkiKallio
Cover Design: Leah Huete

Printed in the USA on acid-free paper.
Order online: www.finishinglinepress.com
        also available on amazon.com

Author inquiries and mail orders:
Finishing Line Press
P. O. Box 1626
Georgetown, Kentucky 40324
U. S. A.

Table of Contents

I. Miss.
A Miss 1
He Reads Heroides 2
Misogyny in Rabelais 3
Elijay Is Not Where 4
What Was Inserted 5

II. Mistakes.
Amiss 9
You See Me, a Woman Flayed 10
What I Wrote While She Was Still Nursing 11
Failure to Yield 12
Things That Should Not Crack Open 13

III. Mistress/Mrs.
I Went Missing 17
Premature 18
Measuring Tape 19
Rebecca Dingley Writes of Stella 20
Cedar Waxwing in Our House 22

IV. Missed.
His Mistakes 25
Violets in Our Yard 26
A Little Cracked 27
A Letter is Nothing Novel 28
De-Extinction Machines 29

For Aurora, always.
And for Elizabeth Kraft and Martine Watson Brownley,
the scholars who helped me find Swift—and Stella.

I. Miss

When Esther Johnson was eight years old, Jonathan Swift took her under his wing. This is and is not something we now refer to as grooming. What woman, man hasn't found her/him-self vulnerable to an authority figure, especially one who is—like Swift—also Other, himself a victim of the same system and of different ones? Sharing in that difference does not make it permissible though, and Stella swiftly becomes pliant, pleasurable because she wants him to see her as more than a child, better than a woman.

A Miss

"Miss,
take
that away."
*(My grandmother was not afraid to send back
the things that she had ordered.
She disordered them.)*

Miss, take me
away.

Take
me,
a miss.

He Reads Heroides

Heroides, he reads you,
each woman ventriloquized,
an act of sexual
                              textual
violence.

Women
overwrought   overwritten.
It's no wonder I'm voiceless
when I   do not
read or
receive their rightings.

Misogyny in Rabelais

When a [male] professor
singles   you
out
for writing a position paper
about medieval misogyny
so that he can explain to   you
that   you
have missed
The Point.

It is not valid
[he says]
to
analyze implicit / explicit structures of gender terrorism
in
Great Literature
because it is
Great Literature
even when a woman is being
raped while onlookers laugh.

He's right since
he is grading   you
so   you
write for him.
He smiles
smugly at how   you
submit.
I make an A in that class by failing   you
myself.

Elijay Is Not Where

Elijay is nowhere,
not where I pick apples now.

We did once, when I   was
                                  was not
afraid
to take a bite.

We left with bags overfilled.
We drove home on roads too
curvy. The bag is empty now.

II. Mistakes

After an absence, Swift returned and found her to be "the most beautiful, graceful and agreeable young woman in England." She moved to Ireland in 1702 so that Swift could protect her and her longtime friend, Rebecca Dingley, and where she became the nexus of intellectual circles.

Amiss

A miss, when it began,
and disorder, something
amiss in me, I thought
                            (he told me).
After I met him,
he tried to fix me
                            (he told me).

I wanted to be what
                            he told me
to be: not amiss like this,
not a mess.

You See Me, a Woman Flayed

> *Last week I saw a woman flayed, and you will hardly believe how much it altered her person for the worse.*
> ~Jonathan Swift, A Tale of a Tub

They saw me,
a woman
flayed.

You will hardly believe how

                            I saw myself

when he treated me that way,
how much it altered
me

                    a person
                    her person
                    mine

for the worse.

I see you

watching
the spectacle of my body
as it's rewritten
remarked
on
by them, after
I stood in front of them,
pilloried.

You read it rightly

                    (past and present tense sound the same,
                    and I mean it both ways).

Still I wonder, worry
about my legibility,
what you see when you read me.

Please read me,
even if my spine cracks under pressure
and I flinch when your eyes linger
too long over the letters like lesions
cut deep in my brain.

What I Wrote While She Was Nursing
> *What is wonderful to conceive, the bulk of Spleen encreased faster than the Sucking could diminish it.*
> ~Jonathan Swift, The Battle of the Books

While my daughter was nursing, I wrote about:
gendered space
the semiotics of servitude
maternal culpability
corporeal intelligibility
domestic economies
embodiment
authority
misogyny
> in Margaret Cavendish, Jane Cavendish, Elizabeth Egerton, Aphra Behn, Henry Fielding, Frances Brooke, Eliza Lucas Pinckney, Janisse Ray.

Swift's Goddess Criticism fed her children on
her spleen, and as if by magic,
it "encreased faster" than they
consumed it or her.

My breasts grew
smaller as she sucked on them.
That was not the only diminishing.
He became less to me
                as she grew,

                              as I grew.
I wore the allusions,
those critical garments,
until they didn't fit any more.

Failure to Yield

What I see when I look
through my windshield
is not this road.

I see what happened to me,
what could have happened to me
if I had taken a different turn
       when two roads diverged,
what could have happened to me
without an airbag:
it saved me but left a burn.

I see what happened to them,
two people I knew well, then not at all.

I check my rearview mirror,
my side mirrors more now
than I did when my father
taught me how to drive.

I frustrated him with my failure
to look around, to move with confidence.
I frustrate myself with my failure
to look see, to let go of old ghosts,
to make the right turns.

Things That Should Not Crack Open

These things have cracked open:
eggs, palms in winter, windows
of a house, windows
of a car,
a car,
the pink bleeding hearts
in our garden
blooming too soon
by the wild violets.

III. Mistress/Mrs.

Swift and Stella fought in 1707 because of Esther Vanhomrigh—the Vanessa of his poems. There was an uneasy triangulation until Vanessa, deathly ill with tuberculosis, told Swift never to see Stella again. She destroyed a will she made in Swift's favor because of their fight. Scholars have argued for years about whether or not Stella and Swift secretly married. She called herself a spinster for her entire life, and Dingley said the two were never alone together.

I Went Missing

It was a miss
take
to
take
his name. I went
missing when I
miss
took
my
self
for his Mistress.

Measuring Tape

You have wasted your
self for her, for
him—expanded where
you would contract.
I encircle you;
I tell that story
of change, even
when you pull me
tight, suck it in,
your waistline,
this wasted line,
           write
in the middle.

Premature

> *Then Cloris her fair Hand withdrew,*
> *Finding that God of her Desires*
> *Disarm'd of all his pow'rful Fires.*
>   ~Aphra Behn, The Disappointment

This will never be my state.

After I left him,
I learned about
the Pride of Wisconsin,
a melon I'd never tried
before moving here for him.
The "fabulous Midwest historic variety"
is shaped
        naturally
like a football
with a hard shell
and such sweet flesh.

Roadside stand food.
The kind that never
disappoints.

My season with it
ended too soon.

Rebecca Dingley Writes of Stella

"I was modest,"
Swift wrote to her.
Was I modest?

"I wish you could hear me,"
Swift wrote to her.
Could he hear me?

He told her his voice
had a cadence of innocence,
"as when little girls say,
'I have got an apple, miss,
and I won't give you some.'"

We ate apples
while he was gone.

We waited for his letters
with our mouths open,
hands open.

"No," he says, "you are not
naughty
at all,
write
when you are disposed."

I taste it, feel the flesh between my lips.

His heart
was at his mouth
he said (for fear).

He wanted her
              my
modesty. A modest proposal
to a
modest poetaster.

Enjoy,
Swift wrote to her,
and do not stop short
"out of modesty."

Cedar Waxwing in Our House

A primordial instinct urges him to catch it.
He carries it inside for us to see it.

His paws and jaws have grown
accustomed to prepackaged prey
like grain-free food by Rachel Ray.
The food comes in a pink bag,
part of the guerilla tactics
responsible pet owners use to
emasculate cats like him.

That is us.

We are
responsible
pet owners.

We are
the people who choose
grain-free cat food and
lightweight litter for
rescued cats we have
neutered. Domesticity
can feel like a form of
terrorism, and sometimes
a feral urge creeps in
on mouse feet or cedar
wax wings.

He caught it.
It escaped.

We are too well-bred to let instinct kick in.
We are domestic cats in a feral world.

The cat's eyes meet mine.
We have green irises encircled in gold.
We look away, embarrassed.

IV. Missed

In her mid-forties, Stella thought she was dying. Her health declined between 1726 and 1728, when she died and an inconsolable Swift wrote The Death of Mrs. Johnson. Swift's Journal to Stella was published posthumously. "Bon Mots de Stella" was the appendix to some editions of Gulliver.

His Mistakes

*He actively avoids
taking
responsibility.*

"Miss
takes
were made."

And a miss
took
him away.

Violets in Our Yard

These flowers defy logic.
They belong to me
in the same way
I belong to this house,
a weed on its edges.

A Letter Is Nothing Novel

Your epistolarity defined me
defines me.

I am an envelope, sent back and forth
between men until the seal breaks
and my signature ends it.
I do not
like
licking
just to be
opened again.

A Little Cracked

On
her
thirty-sixth birthday,
he
told
her
she
had an "angel's face a little cracked." Other women derided
her
("Stella is no chicken").
> There is love in that backhanded compliment, love in the misogyny.
> There is also the backhandedness, the misogyny—how
he
wants
her
to be what
he
knows is inside
her
mind, outside it, and
he
makes
her
know
he
makes
her
meanings.
    e.g. crazy making.

De-extinction Machines

We're terrible readers of cautionary tales.

Jurassic Park	and	Oryx and Crake
masculinist blockbuster	or	feminist speculative fiction
science assumes sex	as	sex assumes science

binary oppositions
make (non)
sense
of mass extinction
                        or simply
of my entropic nerve endings
of my emptied instincts,
        the primitive part. My hypothalamus stopped functioning.

I'm looking for what's been lost: *auroch, bucardo, Carolina parakeet, dodo.*
I'm cataloguing these long-lost bodies alongside my own primal longings.
                                                 I am the chicken
who gave birth
to a
                        peregrine falcon.

Born in Florida but raised in Snellville, Georgia, **Emily Bowles** learned quickly that mermaids melt in the Georgia heat—and that southern culture doesn't always make sense to a vegan feminist, especially one who fell in love too early with Emily Brontë and Emily Dickinson.

Emily studies English at the University of Georgia and completed a PhD from Emory University in 2004, where she learned about women's tenacious, surprising methods of transgression, even under repressive circumstances. Her poetry incorporates her historical research with her lived/living experiences of gendered violence, much of which she began to understand as an advocate and crisis line volunteer for a domestic violence shelter in Wisconsin.

Now, Emily writes poetry while sharing her passions for feminism, sustainability, and wellness as a writer, activist, and educator. She also knits magical creatures and has written a middle-grade novel inspired by *Watership Down*. Find more of her writing at https://embowlden.blogspot.com/.

www.ingramcontent.com/pod-product-compliance
Lightning Source LLC
LaVergne TN
LVHW041601070426
835507LV00011B/1231